Growing Up in Missouri

and Other Short Stories

Nell M. Berry

PublishAmerica
Baltimore

First printing

ISBN: 1-4137-4971-2
PUBLISHED BY PUBLISHAMERICA, LLLP
www.publishamerica.com
Baltimore

Printed in the United States of America

I want to dedicate this book to my parents, Joe and Mary Campbell for the sacrifices they made to raise their family during the Depression of 1929 and beyond.

I also want to dedicate it to my dear brother, Wes, who sacrificed his young years and personal life to be the guardian of a teenager, me.

Last, but not least, I want to dedicate it to my family who has put up with me all these years and still loves me; to my children, who had faith in me when I didn't have much faith in myself. Now, I have learned Who I should have faith in; my Heavenly Father, Who has given me the talent and ability to write these stories; also poems and songs. I give Him all the glory. Thank You Jesus!

I would like to thank my family for being my greatest fans and my son, Nathan for suggesting I write a book about my childhood.

I also want to thank my husband for putting up with me while I struggled to put it together.

I would like to thank Carol Roach, because she encouraged me and because she referred me to Publish America.

I would also like to thank Publish America for publishing my first book.

TABLE OF CONTENTS

INTRODUCTION

I am seventy-three years old and I have been writing poems for a good part of my life; however just recently I decided to try writing short stories. My journey through life has been a long and sometimes difficult one. But with the help of my family and the Lord Jesus Christ, I have come this far and will go on as far as He is willing to use me.

CHAPTER 1

Growing Up in Missouri I
Nell Berry 8/31/03

As I was growing up in Missouri, we moved to a rural community called Dealtown. There was a one room school house there, used for elementary school, grades one through eight. The building was used, too, for a church, a Baptist Church.

I began school there in the first grade. My teacher was Rebecca Cato. I loved Miss Cato. She was a beautiful, slender dark-haired girl, possibly twenty-five years old. However, since I was only six or seven at the time, I really couldn't accurately give her age.

I have two older sisters, Vi, the oldest, being about thirteen at the time. My other sister, Dorothy, was five years my senior, making her about eleven.

When we first began school there, we lived some distance away and had to walk every day close to three miles to and from school. Not many local residents were able to afford an automobile. Most of them were farmers. That was before millionaire farmers.

I remember one weekend my sisters and I were invited to spend the weekend with Miss Cato. She was pretty fond of my sisters and me. So we were very excited to go and spend the weekend with her and her family. She still lived with her mother and father.

While we were there, it was so wonderful to actually have a good meal at breakfast. I suppose we had two or three other meals while we were there but I can only recall breakfast. Being poor, our breakfasts usually consisted of cornmeal mush, oatmeal and once in awhile, eggs, if my Dad had worked for a farmer and was paid for it. There at Miss Cato's, we had bacon, country ham and eggs and toast or biscuits with homemade jelly.

Their house was a typical farm house, with the bedrooms upstairs and kitchen and living room downstairs. No bathroom. Neither was there an outhouse.

There were lots of trees. So we had to go in the woods to "do our morning business," as they used to say when I was a kid.

In the morning, we got up and got dressed and washed our face and hands in a wash pan. No sink— there was a wood range which the meals were prepared on.

The water had to be brought in from a cistern or well in the back yard and heated on the range. I am surprised people didn't get sick from drinking water from those cisterns or wells. But I never heard about it if they did.

That weekend was special to me. I, in a sense, had my teacher, Miss Cato all to myself. Of course, there were my two sisters. But they didn't count. Miss Cato showed me a lot of attention which I did not get from anyone else, attention and affection I needed so desperately. She shampooed my hair and cut it and curled it. My admiration for her grew enormously after that weekend.

It was with great sadness that we received the news the following year that Miss Cato was not going to be our teacher. She had taken a job in some larger city. Replacing Miss Cato was a girl probably younger than Miss Cato, named Leatha Collins.

Miss Collins was just as nice as Miss Cato had been, but for some reason we weren't as close to her. She, too, invited all three girls, my two sisters and me, to go home with her for the weekend. There again, we had wonderful meals. She also lived at home with her mother and father and a brother, Claude.

There was not an indoor bathroom, or even an outhouse there. One morning Claude went out in the woods to "do his business" as they used to say and he came back in cursing to himself, but loud enough for us to hear him. "The damn leaf broke through," was his disgusted comment. There was no toilet tissue either.

This was part of my growing up years in Missouri.

My dad was an uneducated man, who only went through the second grade. He could barely read. But he could do arithmetic and he read well enough to read his Bible. He did the best he knew how. He tried to raise his children according to the Bible.

My dad went hunting and fishing and I remember once he went

out, caught a mess of fish and fried them up for supper.

We didn't have electricity then and we lighted our supper table with lamplight. Someone said pass the biscuits and it didn't clear the lamp as they were passed. In passing the biscuits the lamp was struck and broken and coal oil or kerosene poured into the platter of fish. Our supper was ruined.

We were more careful about passing the biscuits after that incident.

I remember my dad taking us swimming in the river. He would put me on his back and swim across the river with me.

Growing up in Missouri, we had many hardships. Sometimes we had very little to eat and not very good clothes to wear. But we made it. And I don't think we were any worse for the wear. In fact, it might have been good for us, helped form our character. We know what it is to be abased and we know what it is to abound, as Paul says in the Bible. We have learned to be content with whatever we have, not to always want everything that comes out new on the market.

Not that I don't want new things—I prefer having nice things, to be honest. But I could do without if I had to. With God's help, we won't have to go through that again.

CHAPTER 2

Growing Up in Missouri II
Nell Berry 7/31/03

Growing up in rural Missouri in the thirties was a challenge for anyone. But for me it was particularly challenging. I was the last child of the family, the "baby of the family" as I was referred to. My sister Dorothy was five years my senior. My older sister, Violet, was seven years older. We were very poor and my parents were both old in comparison to the parents of the other children. My mother was thirty-eight years old when I was born. My father was forty-six.

There was nothing to do back then for a young child six or seven years old. Not living on a farm, there were no chores to do. My parents could not afford toys therefore we had to create our own entertainment. Sometimes our entertainment was making mud pies, letting them dry and pretending to eat them.

My mother was ill one day and we lived in a one room house, with my two sisters and me and my parents sleeping in that one room; the kitchen, living room and bedroom, all together. As I stated earlier, my mother was ill in bed. There was a noise coming from the inside of the wall and there was nothing but cardboard on the wall to keep out the cold.

My father began tearing the cardboard off the wall to find out what was making the noise.

Turned out to be a snake, a king snake, they called it. I think it was just an old black snake, which isn't poisonous, but my dad killed it anyway. That snake didn't bother us anymore.

We had just come back home from St. Louis, MO, where my dad thought he might be able to find work. That was right after the Depression and there were not a lot of jobs in our area. So we went to St. Louis and stayed with family members while Dad sought employment.

I began school that year in St. Louis, so they took me to one of the local elementary public schools and registered me. I received a vaccination, which I had not had before. It was a new rule that all children had to be vaccinated for diphtheria, tetanus and whooping cough before entering school, if I recall correctly.

Of course, my vaccination was a "lollapalooser," as they used to say, and it was successful. It was very sore and had a huge scab on it, which was normal. The only problem was, someone bumped me and knocked the top off my vaccination. It really bled a lot. So they fixed it by putting some type of guard on it, which I can't remember what it was at this time. It was before plastic.

Soon after that incident, when I had barely gotten to know the names of my classmates, we moved back to our hometown.

Someone had built a one room cabin out in the woods. Even though that is one of the things I can't remember, at the tender age of five, the owner, I'm sure was a friend of my dad's and they let us live there for a time.

I had to walk to school, along with my two sisters, three miles there and three miles back. That is quite a walk for a five year old. Along with their memories not being very good, they aren't too strong either.

That winter was bitterly cold as I recall, and my sisters walked faster than me, and I would be lagging behind, crying and saying "Wait for me." I had to run to catch up with them. That was good, because it warmed me up.

One day in the summer we were walking home from school and we saw a bush shaking as if someone had hold of it and was shaking it for all it was worth. When we got home and told Dad about it, he said it was a snake that had wrapped itself around that bush and was shaking it. I think he called it a spread adder.

The following winter, going to school, my dad had put cardboard in my shoes. (Hooray for cardboard!) He had wrapped my feet in tow sacks to keep them warm. My shoes had holes in them. The cardboard kept the snow out. He made us wear long brown cotton stockings, and long underwear. When we got to school we would roll the stockings down and the long underwear up. Then before we left to go home, we would reverse the process. We were very poor and cardboard was cheaper than new shoes.

Not long after that, we moved to a big, old two story farm house, which was a short distance from the school house. So we didn't have to walk so far to school after that.

The school, a one room school house, had an old time pump organ in it and they had just installed new gas lamps. They were called Aladdin lamps. They really gave out more light than the regular fluorescent lights or a frosted light bulb that we have nowadays.

We drank water from a cistern. In back of the school room, there was another room which was where the cistern was. The *big boys*, eighth graders, were always sent out to get water. They were also sent out to get mistletoe at Christmas time.

My brother and I are the only two left of our family. Those were some difficult but wonderful years; my parents were still alive. It was painful growing up an orphan.

(My brother has since died; the day before my seventy-third birthday, Valentine's Day, he passed away, Feb. 13th, 2004.)

CHAPTER 3

Growing Up in Missouri III
and The Headless Horseman
Nell Berry 9/27/03

Growing up in Missouri, we found many ways of amusing ourselves. We had to, because we didn't have toys, or bicycles, just our imaginations.

There were always stray dogs that someone dropped off at our house. They usually wound up getting killed one way or another. But we played with them when they were around.

My dad didn't know how to treat animals. He was usually very mean to them. Like the kids, he expected them to do as they were told and to speak when spoken to. That's just the way he was brought up and he thought that was the way to do things. He did the best he knew how.

I remember one Halloween, my older sister, Vi, wanted to put sheets on us, to look like ghosts and then hide outside by the house and scare my younger sister, Dorothy. However, when my dad heard about it he wouldn't allow us to do it.

One night, around Halloween, our teacher, Leatha (probably short for Oleatha) Collins, the only teacher in our one room school house, came to visit us and she suggested we take a walk. It was a bright moonlit autumn night and, of course, my two sisters and I were excited to go.

We walked for some distance and then we discovered we were headed in the direction of the old country cemetery. Well, we were a little frightened to go to a cemetery at night. You know, all the stories about ghosts and spirits that were told around Halloween.

But putting on a show of bravado, we wouldn't admit we were afraid. Our teacher, Miss Collins, was only taking us there as a kind of joke. After we were almost in the gate of the cemetery, one of them yelled in a frightened voice, "Here comes the Headless Horseman, Oooohhhh!!!"

You never saw three kids run so fast in your life. Of course, I'm sure my older sister, Vi, and Miss Collins, had this all planned. They ran as fast as my sister Dorothy and I did.

I think they probably scared themselves when one of them let out that scream of terror.

Well, of course, there was no "Headless Horseman" but it sure made for some excitement for a short while. We have laughed about it since then. But at the time, it was scary.

CHAPTER 4

Growing Up in Missouri IV
Nell Berry 10/3/03

I remember "Mama." That was the name of a program on television in the fifties. I wish I could truly say I remember my mama.

The thing I remember most about my mother was that she was frail and looked older than her chronological age and was sick most of the time.

We didn't know what really caused her death. To this day, I don't know for sure. The only cause of death listed on her death certificate was "Inflammation of the brain," whatever that means.

She would be walking down the country road where we lived and would have to sit down on the side of the road to keep from falling. Her head would start to draw backward and if she had not sat down, she would have fallen backwards. I have never read a description of any illness that caused these symptoms.

Mama was not a very strong person physically, but she had a temper, I am told. She was Irish and had the red hair to go with it. She knew my Dad was going somewhere on his way home from work and she had my brother follow him. Turned out he was only stopping off at the local beer joint to swap stories with the guys. But I can imagine what would have happened if she had caught him doing something wrong.

She had had one bad marriage and I don't think she would have hesitated to leave my Dad if he had been doing something she felt was not right.

Her first husband had died of kidney disease, leaving her with two young children. She met and married another man, whose first name was Charles. I don't recall the last name. But he was not good to her two boys and she left him after a short time.

Her oldest son died when he was four years old of pneumonia, I think.

Then she met my father. He saw her getting off a train at the train station and said, "I'm going to marry that woman," which he did. They had four children, and I was the fourth one and I believe she had two stillbirths. She did not have an easy life.

The other thing I remember about Mama was how she rocked me and sang to me when I was little.

I remember when I had the measles; she sat and rocked me all night. At least to my mind at that age, it was all night. It could have possibly been a shorter length of time.

She was a very devoted mother and I miss her to this day. Tragically Mama passed away when I was ten and she was only forty-six years old. She left me, my sister Dorothy, my dad and my older sister Vi, who was already married and had two children of her own and my brother who was in the Army at the time.

I can still see her on the bed. I didn't know it at the time, but she was dying. She had been ill for some time. The doctor must have known she was not going to live and they called my brother home from the service. I believe he was stationed at Fort Benning, GA. We were all standing around the bed—my sister Vi, myself, my dad and my sister Dorothy, watching my brother sitting on the edge of the bed; he leaned over, kissed Mama and as we were watching, I could see the pulse in her neck beating. Then suddenly it stopped. That's when we knew she was gone. I was only ten at the time but I knew my mama was gone. My life was never the same after that.

My half brother, Frankie, died of kidney disease like his father, just two years before Mama at the age of thirty, and my father died one year after she did. I think he died of a broken heart.

CHAPTER 5

Growing Up in Missouri V
Nell Berry 10/6/03

As most of you who have been following my *Growing Up in Missouri* stories, know by now, *I grew up in Missouri.* Back in the 1930's when I was born and grew up, there weren't any concerts to attend, no television and some of us were too poor to own a radio. We didn't have cars for every member of the family as do most households nowadays. In fact, we didn't own a car. The only entertainment we had was when some neighbor stopped by to visit, or when we found some new way to use something that was a common household tool or farm tool.

Kids nowadays have scooters, probably called by a different name now; they have bicycles, four wheelers and they have television, VCRs, DVDs, CDs, computers, GAME BOY, and every other toy or method of entertainment you can possibly think of.

We had to make our own amusement. For example, I remember making mud pies and pretending to eat them after they "baked" in the sun. I remember using the rim of a wagon wheel to roll down the road. We made sticks to guide them with; a stick with a crossbar at the end of it. We made wooden guns, with rubber bands cut from old inner tubes from old tires and a wooden snap clothespin on the handle of the gun, to have cowboy and Indian shoot-outs. Rarely did we have the real toy. It was usually something we thought up ourselves. That was ingenuity and imagination. Kids nowadays have lost that. They don't have to use their imaginations, they don't have to dream up toys to play with; their parents buy them everything their little hearts desire. This is one thing that is wrong with the world today. Kids have too much. They don't lack for anything. That was possibly what formed the character of so many of our inventors and craftsmen of yesterday. They used their imaginations and developed the God-given skills and ingenuity that was used to build the America we know today.

Children of our day had parents who taught them skills, learned from having to use *their imaginations and ingenuity.*

We had storytellers. My dad used to tell us stories. I don't remember too many, because I was too young to take it all in. There was one story he told that used to scare the bejeebers out of me. I don't remember the whole story; just that he saw this big ball of fire coming after him and then it would disappear. This was told at Halloween.

Another story he told at Halloween that I remember was about my grandmother.

She had been doing her evening chores in the same way and same barnyard for many years. But one evening she went out to milk the cows and it was just after dark or right at dusk. Maybe her eyesight was failing, I don't know. She saw something white in the barnyard that she had never seen there before, or that she remembered.

Being superstitious, as many people were in those days, she thought it was a ghost. But she wanted to make sure it was not of human origin. So she attacked it by throwing herself on it.

That was a bad move, because after she nearly killed herself by attacking it, she recalled, it was an old sycamore stump that had been there for years.

I don't imagine she ever forgot that stump again, after she recovered, that is.

Our Uncle Oscar used to come visit us periodically and stay a few days; then he would leave and we never knew where he went or when he would be back.

Uncle Oscar drank pretty much all the time; alcoholic beverages, that is. You couldn't tell he was drunk by his actions or even his speech. But he would be bleary-eyed, or red-eyed. He told us stories also.

I hope I don't offend anyone with this story, because it is about our dear black brothers. It is told in the context of a lot of years ago, when this kind of speech was common.

He said he attended a military funeral where the one being buried was being lowered into the grave by black pallbearers. We always were told that most black people in those days were very superstitious, as were many white people.

To continue; he said just as the casket was being lowered into the grave, someone in the audience who was a ventriloquist, threw his voice into the casket and said, "Let me down easy boys," in a very deep voice. Those pallbearers nearly had a heart attack and dropped that casket and took off running.

Needless to say it disrupted the funeral and they had to get new pallbearers.

CHAPTER 6

Growing Up in Missouri VI
Nell Berry 12/1/03

As I have mentioned, growing up in Missouri was very difficult when I was a child. It was at the end of the Great Depression and though it was after the Depression of 1929, the effects still held many families in its cold steely grip. Our family was no exception. I remember being on relief one time, which is called Welfare now, and we received powdered milk, powdered eggs, Oleo Margarine; at that time it was white and they gave you a little packet of powdered food coloring to mix into the Oleo Margarine to make it look like butter. It was nothing more than pure old vegetable shortening. There were things like a three-pound can raspberry jelly, which I am reminded of to this day by the jelly that is used in jelly donuts. I love jelly donuts, but that raspberry jelly just did not stimulate my taste buds.

Then there were the clothes we received. We were happy to get them. But some of them were from the previous century, I think. There was a pair of high top shoes that laced all the way up past the ankles and they had a two-inch heel on them. Guess who got to wear those shoes to school.

It was fun at first. I was definitely the only one who had shoes like that. So I was pretty proud of them. That is, till we were playing blind man's bluff at recess and the way they knew it was me was to feel my shoes. Then it got to be kind of embarrassing. But I continued to wear those shoes till we were able to afford a new pair.

Of course, we were always receiving hand-me-downs. I received them from my sisters and never had a new coat I can recall, till after my parents died and I stayed with friends in St. Louis for the summer. These friends were friends of my brother's from before he went into the Army. They had heard that my parents had died and Lucretia, the lady who had been a girlfriend of my brother's, invited me to stay with them for the summer. So I left my hometown and went to St. Louis to stay till school was about to begin that year, which was 1941, when my father passed away. While I was there, Lucretia took me shopping and bought me some new clothes. That was my first new coat. I was so proud of that coat. I still remember it. It was a camel colored coat that had a belt and tied around my waist, just like some of the big girls I had seen. Cool!!!

The Christmas before my father died, he had gotten a job as a night watchman at the armory in town. He was making $98 a month; more than he had ever made in his life. He really splurged. He bought us a new rug for the floor, which we had never had before. We also got electricity, which we had never had before. And he bought me a new dress.

But the best thing I remember, my teacher had given me the Christmas tree from our school room and I took it home and decorated it with paper chains. We didn't have lights. So we strung popcorn and the paper chains and hung them on it. The first Christmas tree we had ever had also.

Then, my father gave my sister and me each five dollars to spend on Christmas gifts. That was the most money I had ever had in my life. I still remember what I bought. For my sisters and my sister-in-law I bought each a pair of nylon stockings. For my dad I bought an Old Spice shaving kit with cologne and shaving lotion in it. Oh, I was so full of gratitude and so in awe of being able to buy gifts for others.

It was the most wonderful Christmas I had ever had; to top it off, it snowed that year, so we had a white Christmas. Perfect!

Not long afterward, in fact it was March of the next year, my father passed away, leaving me an orphan.

Times were hard and we had to do with whatever we could get. Money and jobs were scarce. But we made it. Sometimes I think we are better off for the things we didn't have money to buy. We had a roof over our head and clothes on our back. Maybe not the best, nevertheless, we didn't go naked. The best thing was that we had our mom and dad, till that fateful year. But God supplied our needs.

CHAPTER 7

Growing Up in Missouri VII
Nell Berry 1/27/04

When I was very small, about four years old, we moved to a farm which we rented. It was called the Sam Luck place, because of the original owner, I presume.

The house on this farm was a log house. It had a big kitchen which had a bed in it for Momma and Daddy. The rest of the house consisted of one large bedroom, where my two sisters and I slept. In between the kitchen/bedroom and the kids' bedroom, was a breezeway which was open and could have been closed up to make an extra room, if my father or the owner of the house had had the money to do it with.

Then off the side of the kitchen was an enclosure that we called the summer kitchen. That's where we ate in the summer time. It was much cooler; we didn't have air conditioning in those days, not even a fan. The floor was a dirt floor in this summer kitchen. There was a table and benches.

I remember sitting at the table one time eating and I was sitting with one leg drawn up under me. When I got up to go play, I fell. I thought I was paralyzed, not realizing that my leg had gone to sleep from the circulation being cut off while I sat on it. Of course, it eventually recovered the circulation and I was able to walk normally again.

I remember we had an old rocking chair that my dad had repaired and put a tin bottom in it. My older sister, Vi, used to rock with me standing up in the back of it and we would sing.

We didn't have a well or running water at the Sam Luck place. So, I remember my two sisters and I would pull a sled which carried a rain barrel over to the next farm, to get drinking water. There was a spring at the next farm and the water was as sweet as could be. We would draw the water out of the spring and pour it into the barrel and then pull the sled home. It was not easy in the summer, when there was no snow on the ground for the sled runners to glide on. But we got it home, the three of us. I'm sure I was not much help, being only four years old.

Neither did we have an outhouse at the Sam Luck place, nor a bathroom. So we did the best we could. We used the chicken house, and one day I was sitting on the chicken roost, just four years old remember, and I lost my balance, because my feet didn't quite reach the ground. I fell backwards off the chicken roost. It was just a pole from one side of the chicken house to the other.

I still remember Momma turning my little behind over her lap and cleaning me up. I never heard the end (no pun intended) of that one. You know the old saying, "She (expletive) and fell back in it."

There was a picket fence around the yard and one day my sister Dorothy was playing and had on a pair of someone's high heeled shoes that she had found and the heel was off one of them and it was lost in the grass.

Momma yelled at her to come in the house or asked her what she was doing and she said, "I'm gonna fiddle around out here till I find that other shoe heel." She never lived that down either, nor found the other shoe heel.

Once when we were visiting a relative, we kids were playing and someone said something about eating acorns. But one of my cousins said no they would give you diarrhea.

I asked my sister Vi, "Violet, will acorns make you job in your pants?" I don't remember her answer, but I thought they would die laughing at my question. I was still about four years old at that time, also.

Those were some fun times when we were kids, growing up in Missouri.

Even though we were poor as church mice, we still had fun and we still had our parents.

One of my fond memories includes a visit to my mom's first husband's (who died) cousin, Frank. We had to stay all night because of the weather and they had an attic. It was really cold on this particular occasion and we kids got to sleep upstairs in the attic on a feather bed with a feather bed to cover us. This was a treat for us, we

25

had never slept on a feather bed and had one to cover us.

We had to do with what we had in those days. Most people were in the same boat as we were and just "made do," as they used to say.

We called them Aunt and Uncle, even though they were not even related by blood. Uncle Frank and Aunt Mary had very little money either and they had several kids to feed. One of them, the baby, was Mae. When she got mad she would sit in the floor, bend over till her head hit the floor and she just kept banging her head on the floor till she got what she wanted.

CHAPTER 8

The School House
N.M Berry 8/12/03

In the early years of my childhood, growing up in Missouri, we attended school in a one room school house called Deal Town School District.

This school house served as an elementary school, grades one through eight. It also served as a church house. Though I don't recall any, I am sure it served as a meeting house for the community.

Oh the tales that old school house could tell, if it were able and if it were still in existence.

I remember once we had a pie supper at the school. My mother baked a chocolate cream pie for my oldest sister to take and sell. The pies were sold to the highest bidder and the person who bought the pie, also was allowed to eat supper with the one who brought the pie.

My sister sold her pie to a gentleman who had wanted to date her, but hadn't had the nerve to ask. She didn't really want to share the pie with him, but it was the rule, so she did.

After the supper there was a contest to see who had the biggest mouth. I couldn't believe it when my sister won. She didn't appear to have a large mouth, but she won the prize just the same. She was able to put a large kitchen utility spoon, usually used to stir large pots of soup or in making jelly, in her mouth. That's how she won.

The distance from the school house to our house was not too far. In fact, it was not more than a quarter mile. One Sunday night, we had church. I must not have been more than six or seven years old and after the singing, the preacher's sermon was longer than usual and I was very tired. So, I lay down on one of the front benches or pews and fell asleep.

After church was over, Mom and Dad and the rest of the family took off for home. We walked wherever we went in those days. Not too many people had a car. It was probably near midnight when they got home.

That's when they missed me. They looked everywhere. Thinking I was with one of my sisters or with one of our neighbors, they had not missed me till they got to the house.

Meanwhile, back at the church, it seemed to have gotten awful quiet and awful dark. I got up off the bench and ran to the door. It was locked. I panicked. I began to scream and pound on the door till I probably woke some of the dead in the cemetery a mile or so down the road.

The old fellow who usually took care of the school house and cleaned it up and made sure everything was running pretty smooth, was nearly home. His walk home was down a hill to a hollow, or "holler" we called it, and up another hill. He was about halfway home and he was almost deaf, yet he heard me screaming and pounding on the door.

Soon, I heard someone trying to open the door. I stood back. It was Old Uncle Leean Frazell, the school house janitor. He let me out of the door and took me on down the road to my house. My parents were scared and worried but they were glad to see me safe and sound.

From that time till this, I don't ever remember falling asleep in church again.

CHAPTER 9

Unexpected Blessings
Nell Berry 1/19/02

I was pregnant—with my third child. Boy! was I pregnant! My son weighed nine pounds, two ounces

The ob/gyn told me that since I had nursed my first two children and intended nursing this one, the chances of developing breast cancer were practically zero. He said women who nurse their children, seldom if ever develop breast cancer.

Forty plus years later, I went for a routine mammogram and they found a lump about the size of a pencil eraser in my right breast.

Following an ultrasound, I had a biopsy. Diagnosis: Cancer. It was less than two centimeters, but one doctor/oncologist told me there were 500,000 cancer cells in that small tumor.

The doctors I was being advised by had tried to persuade me to take hormone replacement therapy. Ironically, later I was told if I had been taking the drugs they had prescribed, my cancer would have been much worse. I had refused all those years to take it because of the origin of the drug and the side effects. I give God all the glory.

My daughter, Catie and my son, Nath, an anesthesiologist, wanted to be there with me. I was so glad they wanted to be there. My husband would have had to wait alone during my surgery.

I was really surprised at the calm way I received the news.

I was told it was cancer and that I would have to have surgery to remove the cancer and radiation therapy.

Everyone was shocked at how well I was taking the bad news. Before I knew the Lord, I would not have taken it so well.

I didn't want to take radiation, but my son said, "Mom, there are a lot of people watching you." That meant that I should be strong and set a good example. But God's grace and a lot of my friends and

29

church members praying for me gave me great comfort.

I had to go every day for six weeks, except weekends, to the clinic and receive a radiation treatment, which only took about ten minutes total.

It was during this time that Sept. 11, 2001 took place. We were not aware the terrorist attack had occurred that day, till we got to the clinic and everyone was watching the television. I sat down and wept. It was frightening and sad. It was horrifying just to think of human beings committing such a horrible crime against their brothers and sisters of the human race. We were devastated.

We were almost numb from watching the terrible scenes on television. We couldn't NOT watch it. Yet it was so sad to hear of the many thousands who never made it out alive. Those who went to work that day, expecting to see their loved ones that night and never made it out of that terrifying moment of time. "God," we thought, "what horrible demon has been released?"

As the days went on and fall dragged into winter, my husband and I stayed at our son's house. We went home on weekends.

Also staying with our son and his wife was Lucy, a Chinese student and new Christian, who my son and his wife asked to stay with them while she was going to college. She began to call us Grandma and Grandpa.

Lucy was an angel. She wanted to do everything for us. Even though she was working after class every day, she would come home and fix dinner for us. We had never met anyone like Lucy. She was such a blessing from God.

Another blessing was the fact that my oldest granddaughter, Laura, who had just moved back home from New York, wanted to drive me to the clinic, to give Grandpa a break, so he could go duck hunting.

Spending time with Laura, my son and his wife and grandsons was another blessing. My daughter-in-law, Cyndi, did everything in her power to make me as comfortable as possible. She took me shopping and bought looser fitting bras and tee-shirts and nightgowns so I would be more comfortable.

She was so sweet to me.

Finally, the Lord gave me several poems during that time. I mentioned to the girls at the clinic that I write poetry. I told them I had written one about the 9/11 tragedy and they wanted to read it. So the next day I took a stack of my poems in for them to read and the receptionist, Rose, made a small booklet of them and put them in the waiting room for the patients to read. They seemed to be encouraged and uplifted by them.

Rose framed the 9/11 poem and put it on the bulletin board. One of the girls, a technician named Lori, emailed my poem to a radio station for them to read. They said they would read it. But I wasn't home to listen to the radio, so I don't know if they did or did not.

God is so good. In any situation, whether it is good or bad, He can turn curses into blessings. In any other time of my life, I would have considered my being diagnosed with cancer to be a tragic situation. However, God showed me that you can receive blessings from every situation if you just allow Him to use you and bless you as well.

I feel my son's words to me, "Mom, there are people watching you," were the words that changed my life.

In another situation, my son also made a difference in my life. His father, my husband, of fifty years at that time, was having triple bypass surgery and my son, Nathan, who is a doctor, told me I "had to be strong for Dad." He said, "You can't go in there and break down. You have to be strong for Dad." Of course my son knew me and he knew I was not very strong when it came to a crisis.

Nevertheless, I prayed and asked the Lord to help me be strong and not to break down.

I went into his room where he was waiting to go in for surgery and I never shed one tear. It was amazing, to say the least. In most cases like this I would have been a basket case; but not this time. I was really shocked that I was so calm.

However, it was my son's words that rang in my ears, "Mom you have to be strong for Dad," that helped me, along with the prayers.

That was four years ago. My husband and I will be married fifty-four years in June.

Bio: I am a wife of one husband for fifty-four years, mother of four, grandmother of nine. I love to write poetry, song lyrics and now short stories. I like to sew, cook, and crochet. I am helping in a ministry of a pro-life group called Children of the Heart ministries. I crochet baby blankets, which the founder, Betty Bailey, offers to the ladies or young girls who are persuaded not to have an abortion. This ministry is based in Wichita, Kansas and they could use help. Her email address is bbbailey@mail.mylifeline.net she also has a web site called childrenoftheheartmin.

I love to go to church and sing in church. We attend Perry First Baptist Church in Perry, MO. We live on a small farm on Mark Twain Lake in Missouri.

CHAPTER 10

Entertaining Angels
Nell Berry 11/21/03

I used to be very uncomfortable around people who are mentally challenged. I didn't know how to converse with them. I was afraid I would say something stupid and hurt their feelings. Many of them are more aware of what is going on and can converse as well as a young child. We knew some folks, long ago, who were blessed with a Down's syndrome child. I say blessed because they are the most loving children you could ever want to know. I asked the mother of this child , "How do you talk to them?" in my ignorant, uninformed way. She replied, "Just like you would anyone else."

Since that time, we have gotten acquainted with another family who has a Down's syndrome child and she is the most loving child. Every time she sees us, my husband and I, she will come up to us and give us a hug and kiss.

When I first got to know the family, I was babysitting in the nursery at church one Sunday and this special child was in the nursery. She could be very difficult when she was scared or angry, not knowing what to do with her emotions.

There was one person who could calm her down, though. That was her brother. She seemed to relate to him better than anyone else. He was in the nursery also, but only to take care of his sister. However, he was very helpful, because that day she was not going to stay in the nursery, that is till her brother came. Then she was perfectly alright.

Not long after that incident, we had a carry-in dinner at church and, (I will call her Tracy) Tracy saw my husband and ran up to him and said, "Hi, Kaffidy." No one knew where she got that name. Since then she has called him "Kaffidy."

My husband became so fond of Tracy that last year for her

birthday, he built her a toy box, which was also a seat. She doesn't show too much emotion about those kinds of gifts.

Tracy has a dog she has named Oscar. Oscar seems to know she is special. He does whatever she tells him to do. He is a really small dog, breed unknown. But he is very intelligent.

Whenever Tracy sees me or my husband, she immediately comes over and gives us a big hug. I told her, "I look forward to those hugs." So now she gives me a kiss too.

Tracy enjoys going to the Special Olympics for special children. She participates and last year she won several medals. She was so proud of those medals. Everyone was congratulating her and she loved it.

She is a very special little girl and the whole congregation really loves her.

I believe these children were put here for a reason. God wanted to show us what unconditional love is and they are the perfect example, outside of Christ and His dying on the cross for our sins. They don't care what you look like; if you had two heads; or if you look like Shrek, the ogre in the animated cartoon movie; or if you wear the latest fashions; or if you speak good English, they still love you. They are LOVE personified. When we love them and cherish them as a valued human being, we are entertaining angels.

CHAPTER 11

Friendship
Nell Berry 9/5/03

Many people do not realize you must cultivate a relationship to have a lasting and meaningful friendship. I had very few friends until recently, when it became completely clear, there must be give and take on both sides. People want to be friendly and most seek the friendship of others. However, if there is something in the character that puts people off, the friendship never develops.

There is something in my character that has caused me to lose a lot of friends. It is called poor self esteem. I continuously question the motives of people who want to be my friends. I am always wondering if they are really sincere. I have this terrible pessimistic attitude about myself. My husband says I am the most negative person he knows, because I am always putting myself down and being so hard on myself.

That's a terrible thing, if you have passed it down to your children especially. My children all have a problem, I believe with self worth or low self esteem, with the exception of our two sons, Louis and Nathan, who have learned who they are in Christ. In the early years they, too, were affected by low self esteem. If one knows his place in God's Kingdom, he doesn't have a problem with low self esteem, because he knows ultimately, that's all that counts in this world and the next.

I have come to the conclusion that people do not want to be around a person who is continuously putting themselves down. Therefore, I have decided to let my actions speak for themselves; not to worry about what other people think; to allow them to think whatever they choose, because if I do my best to make friends and I am sincere in my motives, people will want to be my friend.

When my oldest daughter was in second grade, she had a teacher who was not the sweetest person in the world. She was very unreasonable and my daughter did not know why. Mrs. Green, not her real name of course, was a very sour, unyielding individual. Nothing Denise could do was good enough for this teacher. She tried to be helpful and pleasant, but this teacher never yielded. Denise came home in tears and saying she hated this teacher. My daughter was quite hurt.

She began to tell me how Mrs. Green didn't like her, no matter what she did. My daughter was usually very pleasant and most people liked her. I said to her, "Maybe there is a special concern in this lady's life that is causing her grief."

She did not know what I was talking about of course.

I said, "Denise, why don't you try to find out what is bothering Mrs. Green that possibly could cause her to be so disagreeable? Just try to be nice to her and be as pleasant and agreeable as you possibly can. Be more helpful; do special kindnesses for her. Maybe you will find she has personal problems causing her to be this way."

Some time after that, Denise came home and said, "Mom, you were right. I found out Mrs. Green has an invalid husband at home and every day at lunch time and in the evenings, she has to go home and take care of him."

One day at the school's annual picnic that was held in the park in town, I met Mrs. Green. She could not say enough about how kind and how sweet my daughter was. She said, "She is the sweetest child and so helpful and kind."

Denise never had another unkind word to say about Mrs. Green. They became close friends.

I have found it to be my experience, if there is some tragic circumstance surrounding an individual, they are apt to be very unreasonable and unfriendly. Just as my low self esteem has caused me to lose friends and not develop close relationships over the years, in that same way this teacher of my daughter's was so troubled about her circumstances that she was very unpleasant and hard to get along with.

In reality, she was a wonderful person who just needed some kind words and compassion from others.

Of course, I believe my low self esteem stems from the fact that my parents died and left me an orphan at a young age. I have always felt the pain of rejection. I suppose in my immature mind, my parents had abandoned me and that was a form of rejection. Hence my low self esteem.

In conclusion, I strongly believe if we are sincere in our efforts to acquire friendships and keep them; if we show love and compassion for others; if we are not so wrapped up in ourselves and are always open to the kindness of other people, we will develop deep and abiding friendships. These are my own observations.

CHAPTER 12

In The Presence of Angels
Nell Berry 2/16/03

There have been many times in my life when I feel there were angels all around. Once when I was a child, a family friend escorted me home through the woods at night when I got homesick while staying with other friends. He could have done whatever he chose to me. There was no one to stop him. But I felt warm and safe with him holding my hand. I still remember the moon being very bright and it was just a very memorable moment in my life. This friend died not long after that. I was very sad. But even though he was not a Christian, he was a very kind and sweet old man. The whole community loved him. I know there were angels all around that night.

Then there was the time when my husband and I had gone visiting and came home and I was, and still am a coffee drinker. I wanted a cup of coffee before going to bed. I turned on the burner on the electric range under the glass coffee pot to heat a cup of coffee which was left over from dinner.

Hours later, I was sleeping and suddenly, without a sound to waken me, I was wide awake. I raised my head and looked towards a glow in the hallway on the door of the linen closet. I did not immediately recognize where it was coming from. I got up from my bed and went towards the hallway, where I saw the reflection of a red glow on the varnished door of the closet. Immediately, when I got to the kitchen, where the reflection was emanating from, I knew what had happened. I had gone to bed and forgotten to turn off the burner on the electric range. It must have been a comical site, if someone had been watching me. I picked up the now dry coffee pot and didn't know what to do with it. I did a sort of dance, trying to decide where to set it down. I knew if I set it down on a cold surface, it would break into a million pieces. Finally I had the presence of mind to set it back on the burner, which by this time had cooled. But it was too late for the glass coffee pot. It cracked instantly, completely covering the entire glass surface with cracks. Thank the good Lord; it didn't shatter, as I was afraid it would.

I still believe there were angels all around that night, watching out for me and my family. A fire could have resulted from that foolish mistake. But an angel wakened me out of a deep sleep.

Every one of my children, now grown, had serious accidents which could have been fatal. Our oldest son, who is a preacher/ carpenter, has had several accidents which in one instance being thrown out of the bed of a pickup truck, he was in and out of consciousness for several days with a concussion. But an angel was watching over him and preserved his life.

Our youngest son was with our oldest son in one accident in which a fifteen-year-old boy was driving the other car, with his grandparents and several people. These people and the two of them could have been killed. No one was injured. Again I believe an angel was watching over them. They were both spared. Our youngest son had a bruised elbow. He was also in an accident with his grandmother in which her car was totaled and neither of them was injured except for bruises.

In another incident he, our youngest son, was coming home for the weekend from college. He had three other students with him and he swerved to miss another car that was trying to pass illegally on an icy road. He went out of control on the ice and flipped the car. No one was injured. Just the car was a wreck.

Our oldest daughter was hit several times in her car, being propelled into the lane of oncoming traffic by a pickup truck, which got out of control on a rain slick pavement. She wound up with her car wrapped around a pillar of one of the overpasses of Highway 70 in St. Louis, MO. It took two hours to cut her out of her car. She escaped with only superficial cuts and bruises. Yes, it was an angel who was protecting her, in my opinion.

Our youngest daughter was a passenger in a car when it was broadsided on the passenger side and she had a slight concussion and a banged up eye which looked like she had a golf ball in place of her eye only it was purple and black and blue instead of white. There again, I firmly believe there was an angel watching over her.

All my life, I have had the hand of God on me, protecting me from certain disasters. I know that, now that I am older and look back.

There have been many times in my growing up years I could have had disasters befall me. But God or one of His angels was there to protect me.

God has something planned for each of us and He does protect us. But after awhile, if we keep rebelling against Him, our protection runs out. If we live for Him and try to stay in His will, we will be protected until He wants us to come to live with Him in Heaven.

CHAPTER 13

Unfulfilled Love
Nell Berry 1/4/04

How many times as a young girl growing up did I get my heart broken? Every time I met a boy and went out with him, if I liked him and he liked me seemingly, I fell madly in love with him.

I'm sure I am not the only woman who has had this experience.

There was Tim when I was nine years old. He was the younger brother of Ralph who was madly in love with my sister Vi at the ripe old age of fifteen. Lordy me, I was so enamored of Tim. Once when my sister wanted to see Ralph, she allowed me to accompany her and we walked (not having transportation in those days, our feet were the best vehicle we had) six miles to the church where Ralph and Tim were attending. It was as the song goes, "The Church in the Wildwood." After having walked all that distance, we were tired. But having gotten there, my sister was not too interested in the church service, especially when she saw Ralph.

Our church service consisted of sitting in Ralph's car, he was fortunate to have one, and the two of them were what they called "necking" at the time. I don't know what they call it now. In fact, they don't have anything close to "necking" as far as I can see nowadays. It's more like trying to swallow each other's tongue. Disgusting!! Don't they know they can contract all kinds of diseases that way?

Getting back to Tim, he was so cute, ten years old, and I can't remember what he looked like now. But boy at that time in my life he was a "cool dude," another colloquialism I am familiar with, but do not know the rudiments of. Anyway, he was cute. If my dad had known I was in the backseat of a car with a boy, just getting to know each other, mind you, he would have tanned my hide but good, and my sister's for being the instigator of the situation.

Then there was Floyd. Oh my, what Floyd did to my blood pressure I will never tell!! I was about eleven at that time. Of course, at that time I didn't even know I had a blood pressure.

There was Howard, and Glenn, Elmer, Dub, Joe, John, and several I have forgotten the names of.

Then there came my future husband. I can't even describe my feelings for him. He had blond curly hair, kind of long for that era and six foot two, eyes of blue. But what I really fell for was his sense of humor. He was always clowning around. Never a dull moment while I was with him. Until he took me home. Then it was all serious, he was madly in love with me and I with him.

We met at the public library. We were both fifteen. He was with a group of kids and I was with a group of my friends. He just swept me off my feet. Of course he wanted to take me home from the library and I consented.

In 1949 on Valentine's Day I was nineteen years old; he gave me my engagement ring that night.

That was fifty-three years, four kids and nine grandchildren ago, and we still love each other. We haven't had a perfect marriage. It has been a lot of "trouble and toil," as they say. But all in all, it has been worth it. I love my children and grandchildren with everything that is in me and even my son-in-law and two daughters-in-law.

Soon we may be starting on the next generation. Our granddaughter is getting married in June. We also have one grandson who is married for about four years. He just told us recently that we are going to become great grandparents in September

I just give God all the praise and honor and glory for keeping us together and well all these years. Except for a triple bypass surgery my husband is in pretty good health and I have survived a bout with breast cancer. Praise be to God. Bless His holy name.

My husband says he is going to be duck hunting when he is eighty-five, be the good Lord willing.

CHAPTER 14

A Special Kind of Love
NM Berry 7/22/03

I guess you had to be born before the 1940's to know what I mean about a special kind of love.

My mother and father were both born in the late 1800's and they were of an era when people in their particular part of the country did not demonstrate their feelings too often. When they did it was almost imperceptible.

I remember once when I was about eight or nine years old, I came home from school one afternoon and asked my mom if I could attend a movie which was being shown at the library. Now, we lived on the east side of the river, which was not the best part of town. But in order to get to the library, we had to walk across town and then across the bridge into the main part of the town before turning on Main Street and walking another block or two to reach the library. This was quite a distance for an eight or nine year old.

Naturally my mother said "No." I begged and pleaded and she didn't budge an inch. Finally in rebellion, I said, "I'm going." She warned me what would happen when I got home. But I was determined to go see the movie.

So, off I went to the library. I can't even tell you what the movie was about, because I was so worried that when I got home my dad was going to tan my hide.

I arrived home just at dusk, not quite dark, but so close you could barely tell the difference.

I began to beg my mom not to let my dad whip me. I had seen him give whippings and I didn't want any. Not that he was a child beater. But he made a believer out me.

He never did give me a whipping, but I was so afraid he was going to I never did anything like that again.

That was a special kind of love. They loved me enough not to allow me to do things that would be potentially harmful to me.

I don't remember either my mom or dad ever embracing me and telling me they loved me. However, one day, my father took me to town with him and when we were crossing the street in front of the bank, we met an old friend.

My dad said the usual hellos, how are you, etc. Then he put his arm around my shoulders and said, "This is my baby."

That was the closest thing to an embrace and affectionate hug my dad ever gave me. It was also the closest he ever came to saying he loved me.

But it was a special kind of love. He didn't have to tell us kids that he loved us, we knew it.

However, I do not advocate parents being this distant from their children.

That was the way my father and mother were raised, and they didn't know how to show their love and affection. But children need that show of affection and to be told they are loved often.

As a result of my parents' seemingly cold and distant ways toward me, I was unable to show my love and affection to our children. Therefore, it was hard on them. They had a difficult time with that.

So please, parents, show your love and affection for your children. They will reward you for it after they are grown and have children of their own.

CHAPTER 15

A Question of Courage
NM Berry 8/1/03

My husband loves to fish and duck hunt. He will go fishing or duck hunting regardless of weather.

He hasn't changed, as far as his love of fishing and duck hunting, in the fifty-three years we have been married. However, Lou has changed his priorities. He goes to church on Sundays and any other day or night of the week there is church and anything related to church. Two heart attacks, one only four years ago, which resulted in triple bypass surgery, haven't slowed him down, as far as fishing and hunting. He has slowed down to a degree, in the sense that he is physically unable to do some things because of his arthritis. But it hasn't stopped him from doing what he loves and thinks he must do.

I suppose it's forward to boast about my husband. Of course, without God we are nothing. But I am very proud of my husband. I am not going to lie and say we never have an argument, we are human. However, that does not keep me from being proud of him.

Lou has a weakness for young people. He will go out of his way to be helpful and kind to them. Just a couple of weeks ago, he volunteered as a counselor at the Baptist youth camp. There was one little fellow he developed a soft spot for. This little guy's name was Jabez, unusual to say the least. That is what drew Lou's attention at first. But then he just really got attached to him because of his sweet nature. He is still talking about Jabez.

A few winters ago, Lou got acquainted with a couple of the young men at church, I think at that time they were thirteen and fourteen. They were cousins and Lou took a great liking to them. So after asking them if they liked hunting ducks, he asked their parents if he could take them duck hunting with him. Since I am not crazy about the idea of his going out on the lake alone, I was thrilled that he had someone to accompany him.

For several years he took them both duck hunting with him and they really enjoyed themselves. They helped him carry his gun and his duck decoys and he would have a treat for them, such as hot chocolate that he heated on an oil heater he had to heat the duck blind. Well, I guess that was the best time of his life, except when he used to take his own sons duck hunting.

Last winter was a trying time for Lou. One day in December, the 20th to be exact, he was with a young fellow who had asked him to go duck hunting with him. As they were coming back in, they had pulled the boat out of the water and were getting ready to leave, and my husband heard a faint cry for help. He did not know at the time what it was. But after he listened and told his companion to listen, they both decided it was someone crying out for help.

Since they had just about gotten the boat ready to leave, they had to put it back in the water and go out again in the direction of the cry for help and begin looking. They couldn't find anyone. They kept looking and the wind was blowing pretty hard and the water was very rough, so it was difficult to hear. My husband is hard of hearing anyway. But the other fellow heard it and they looked over towards what turned out to be a capsized boat. At first, they couldn't tell it was anything but a stump. Then they saw a hand come up and heard the faint cry again.

There, hanging onto his capsized boat by his fingernails, was a fellow who would not have lasted another fifteen minutes had they not found him. They had to physically pull him into their boat, because he was so weak, he could not help them. Finally they got him into the boat and took him back to the boat ramp. When they pulled the boat out and got him out of the boat, he was so weak he could not walk alone. He was extremely cold from being in the cold water. They had to strip him down to his underwear and put the heater on in his truck and they waited till he was alright. Then they left.

They never even thought to get his name. But I am quite sure this young man would be the first to tell you, he had experienced an act of courage.

Lou came home from that duck hunting experience pretty shook up. Later we were about to eat supper, when the phone rang. It was dusk and the sun had just slipped below the horizon. Lou answered the phone. I could hear someone on the other end of the line screaming into the phone. It was our neighbor Jeannie. "Lou, could you come QUICK, I can't get Larry to answer me."

Her husband, Larry, had been deer hunting on their neighbor's property. She watched him drive slowly from his deer stand to their house. He drove up the incline in front of their house and never got out of the truck, motor still running.

Well, Lou hurried over there and tried to arouse Larry. He tried giving him CPR, Larry still behind the wheel. But it was no use. Jeannie called 911, but the EMT with the ambulance told my husband Larry was already gone when he drove into the driveway.

It truly affected Lou. He and Larry had gotten to be quite good friends. Now, all he could do was remember his friend, walking across our yard, shirttail flapping in the breeze, just to talk or for some advice on a woodworking project. Larry made his living doing wood crafts.

That experience taught Lou the value of friendship. He now talks about how important it is to develop friendships and be a good friend to your fellow man. Especially if that is your neighbor.

CHAPTER 16

Going Back Home
Nell Berry 6/13/04

I was born and grew up till I was twelve years old, in a little town in Southeast Missouri called Poplar Bluff. I have never gotten the true story of how it got the name. It had to do with some bluffs that you could see from the east side of the Black River, I believe.

When we lived there it was a town of over 15,000 population. Living in Poplar Bluff in those days was unique possibly only because that's where I lived. I'm sure there were, and still are, towns that are similar in character and size. But to me it was unique.

We were the poor of the general population. In those days it was not uncommon to be poor. It was during and right after the Depression. There was no work for many people. My father was not an educated man and so he found it difficult to find work. The only work he ever knew was hard labor; on the railroad as a switchman or a yardman; helping farmers plant or harvest their crops for a portion of the harvest or a ham to feed his family.

Once he was paid for his labor in potato sacks full of black eyed peas. We ate black eyed peas till they were coming out of our ears, so to speak. I still love black eyed peas. That was before we moved back into town. In town he found it even more difficult to get work.

I didn't really get to know my parents before they were taken prematurely in death. My mother was at one time a very beautiful lady; small frame, red hair and the palest of blue eyes. Of course, to me she was wonderful, she was my mother. My most prominent memory of her was when I was very young and had the measles. It seemed to me she held me and rocked me all night long on one occasion.

Then there was the time we had to move out of our house because of the flood which occurred every spring for many years, until they built a levee on the river to hold back the water. My mother was ill at the time and they came and took us out of the house by boat.

Once when I was about eight years old, I came home from school one day and asked Momma if I could go to the library which was on the west side of town across the river. She said no, for me to wait and ask my father. But I couldn't wait. I said, "I'm going," and I took off. When I got home it was almost dark; too dark for a child my age to be out alone. My father was not home yet and Momma told me, "You're going to get it when Daddy gets home."

I began to plead with her, "Please don't tell him, Momma. I won't do it again," afraid of what I was "going to get", because I had seen him whip my sisters, and I knew it was not funny. Not that he beat them mercilessly. But they knew it when he gave them a whipping. My older sister, Vi, once remarked, "He just hit the tail of my dress and it didn't hurt." But she cried like it hurt, because she knew if she didn't cry he would keep whipping her till it did hurt.

When my father came home, I just knew I was really "going to get it." But though he promised it, he never did whip me. Just the thought of him whipping me was enough. I never did that or anything "bad" again while they were alive.

I was so grateful to have my parents for as long as I did. But my mother passed away when I was at the tender age of nine. One year later almost to the day, my father had a heart attack and died. So I was left an orphan. My brother, who was eleven years older than I, took me and raised me till I was married at the ripe old age of nineteen.

Many years later, when all my children were grown, except our youngest daughter, who was fifteen at the time, I took them all back to where I grew up on the east side of town. I showed them the school where I went to the fourth, fifth and sixth grade. I had always thought of the school as being a pretty big building. But when I took my kids back there, it was a very small building. I hardly recognized it.

Then I took them to the neighborhood where I grew up till I was twelve. My father had passed away and I was living with my sister-in-law while my brother was overseas during World War II.

The only way I can describe it was a feeling that I had lost my parents all over again. I cried uncontrollably. My children didn't understand why I was crying. I don't really understand it either. But it was like my heart was broken. Everything was different; the house I was born in; the house in which I lived with my parents after my sister got married, which was when she was sixteen; the house in which my sister-in-law and I lived while my brother was in the army, nothing was the same. I lost my childhood there and it was so painful. It was like looking for a family member and finding out they have passed away.

So, the old adage "you can't go home again" is really true, because nothing stays the same. But it's as if I lost it all again, in "going back home."

CHAPTER 17

Christmas Past
Nell Berry 12/2/03

When I was a child, money was scarce. We didn't get new toys for Christmas. If we got a bag of candy with fruit and nuts with it, that was a good Christmas for us.

I remember one year, I must have been about eight years old, and my sister Vi had been dating this young fellow. Actually he was several years her senior. He had come to the house to visit our family, of course mainly to see my sister. This was on or around Christmas Eve.

I suppose he was trying to make a good impression on the family because he brought some gifts. I only remember what he brought me. It was a box of chocolates and the box was the shape of Santa Claus. I think that was the first gift I ever received from anyone outside the family. I kept that box for the longest time. It was definitely the first box of chocolates I ever received.

Years later my husband gave me a box of candy for my birthday, in the shape of a heart, because my birthday is on Valentine's Day. I think I still have that box somewhere with mementos in it.

When my brother was in the service and my dad had gotten the first real job he had ever had in my memory, as night watchman at the armory in our town, my brother got a furlough that Christmas and came home. He arrived in the middle of the night and the door was locked, I think. Anyway, my dad was at work and my sister Dorothy and I were at home alone. This was a year or less after my mother passed away. My sister was about fifteen or sixteen and I was about ten. We heard someone at the door and we were frightened half out of our wits.

We just knew it was an intruder.

When we saw that it was our big brother, home for the holidays, we were so thrilled; both of us began to cry because we were so happy. He was our hero.

The first Christmas after my brother left to go overseas, which had to be about 1941, because my dad had passed away the previous March, I was living with my brother's wife of only about six months. I actually got to buy gifts for my sisters and my sister-in-law. I had been receiving an allowance from my sister-in-law for doing chores after school and I had saved my money, which was only $1.50 a week. But that was a lot of money for me, who had never received an allowance before. I bought my sister-in-law cologne and she gave me a charm bracelet. I was just ecstatic to receive a gift of any kind.

That was the year the song "White Christmas" came out, if my memory serves me right. Every time we would go to town we would hear that song by Bing Crosby. I just loved that song. "Silver Bells" by Doris Day also came out that year and it, too, was one of my favorites.

God is so good. He kept me all those years growing up in Missouri. He provided a home for me and I never had to go to an orphanage.

I am just so grateful to God for giving me a brother who had a good heart and raised me to adulthood. He was only twenty-four years old at the time and he was not thrilled to be saddled with a teenager. But he did it and I will be eternally grateful.

CHAPTER 18

Christmas 1963
Nell Berry 12/11/03

I would like to tell you about the year of the bear. It was also the same year President John F. Kennedy was assassinated.

In the month of November, the 22nd to be exact, I had gone shopping at Kroger's Supermarket and as I was checking out, the manager of the store came up and offered to help me out with my groceries. He was putting them in the back of my station wagon when he made the observation that it sure looked like a storm was brewing. The sky was really dark; I was a little worried about driving home.

However, I had no choice, so I got in the station wagon and started for home.

As I drove in the driveway, it began to rain. My husband was working the second shift at McDonnel-Douglas Aircraft so he was babysitting our youngest son, Nathan. He was just three years old and I was four months pregnant with our fourth child. The two oldest children were in school.

As I walked in the door, my husband had been watching television and I heard Walter Cronkite say, "Interruption! It has just been reported that the President has been shot in Dallas. No further details are known at this time. Repeating: The President has been shot in Dallas, Texas."

I was so shocked I didn't know what to do. My husband brought the groceries in out of the station wagon and we just waited till we heard the rest of the news which said, "The President is dead."

Our hearts were breaking.

What followed, of course, was the analysis of what had happened; then the funeral which was so sad. All I could think was how Jackie must have been feeling and those two little kids would have to grow up not knowing their father. I just cried and cried.

Then it was December of 1963. We had gone shopping at one of the discount stores and did not know what to get the kids for Christmas.

While we were there, we found this brown bear, which was about a foot tall and about fourteen inches long. It was on rollers and there was a rifle with it which shot rubber darts; the kind that create a vacuum when they hit something and stick to it. One was supposed to shoot the darts at the bear and when it was hit, it would change direction and scream a very loud painful cry.

We had already gotten our gifts for the two oldest children, but we were at a loss as to what to buy for our youngest son, Nathan, who was only three years old. When we saw that bear, we just knew he would love it.

We also had bought a little train that ran around on a small track.

Nathan was the kind of kid that couldn't wait till Christmas morning when we opened the gifts. He would wake up early, and I mean early, before daylight, and go in the living room and do the shake, rattle and roll deal with the gifts under the tree, trying to figure out what they were. Then he would wake us up and want to open the gifts.

My husband always took movies at Christmas time. He lined us all up in the kitchen or hallway and had us come in one at a time and took our picture as we came into the living room.

Nathan just couldn't wait. He was always the first one in line.

When he opened his gifts we were expecting him to really be happy with the bear.

He opened it and didn't really know what to do with it.

Then our son Louis took the rifle and began to shoot the bear with the darts. As he shot the bear and it began to scream and go in the direction of Nathan, he ran the other way. He was so frightened of the bear.

My husband took movies of this and to this day we look at those movies and nearly roll with laughter at our son running from that stupid bear. He laughs at it now, he has kids of his own. But he didn't think it was so funny then.

He never did play with that bear. We finally gave it away.

That same year, we were undecided about what to give our

thirteen-year-old daughter, Catie. Finally we decided that since she was starting junior high school, she would need some new clothes. So we decided to give her a check.

We wrote the check out and pinned it to the Christmas tree.

When she didn't get any Christmas presents that year, she was devastated. Finally she found the check pinned to the Christmas tree and she was not *so* unhappy. But she still was not happy about it. Getting a check instead of gifts was not her idea of a good Christmas.

We never did that again. She was so disappointed, it broke my heart.

In April of that following year our fourth and last child was born, a blond haired, blue eyed baby girl. She was so precious. I had not wanted another baby. But when she was born, I loved her instantly and was so proud of her. We named her Deneen.

CHAPTER 19

Christmases Remembered
Nell Berry 12/30/03

When I was a child growing up, I can't recall ever having a Christmas tree at home. We had huge ones at school, the one room schoolhouse I attended from the first to the fourth grade.

Of course, there was no electricity out in that area of Dealtown, MO, so we did not have Christmas lights on it.

The first Christmas tree we had in my recollection was the one given to me on the last day of school at J. Minnie Smith School in Poplar Bluff, MO before Christmas vacation, by my fourth grade teacher. We decorated it with red and green paper chains made of construction paper and we strung popcorn and hung on it also. There were other various ornaments which my sister and I made but I can't remember what they were.

During the years of my children growing up, we had several trees of various species, such as one that was an aluminum one and we did not care for that one. The other trees we bought were usually Scotch pine. We bought one that we wanted to plant after Christmas in our yard, but it did not survive.

When we moved here to the farm several years ago, our first Christmas our son-in-law and our two sons went out in the field and cut down a cedar tree. They are very pretty at first, but soon begin to dry out.

Anyway, my daughter Catie, being one who loves tradition and old fashioned Christmases, wanted to make it look authentically country or old fashioned. She suggested we string popcorn and cranberries, as well as making paper chains to hang on it.

That is what we did. It looked so pretty. I crocheted some ornaments to hang on it and we bought a few old-time looking ones at the dime store. I can't remember if we strung lights on it or not.

Nevertheless, we got it looking pretty old fashioned.

The next morning we looked at the tree and something had eaten the popcorn off of it.

This house we live in is an old farmhouse and that was before we did extensive redecorating. No one had lived in this house for over ten years and there were definitely signs of deterioration from the weather and from not being lived in. One of the signs of deterioration were holes big enough to throw a cat through, through which field mice could and did make their entrance.

Apparently they were hungry mice, because they ate the popcorn off the tree. They probably ate some of the cranberries, too.

However, the old fashioned tree and ornaments served their purpose for the few days we kept it up and since then we have not had a cedar tree. Nor have we had popcorn strung on one and no mice have been invited. Sometimes they come even if they aren't invited, though. We have plugged up all the holes they used as entryways but somehow they still find a way to get in once in awhile.

Just this year, the last week before Christmas, my husband and I were sitting at the dining room table one morning and out came a mouse from the back of the wood stove. I did what any red blooded American grandmother would do; I screamed and drew my feet up off the floor and my knees up to my chin.

My husband did what any red blooded American grandpa would do and saw the mouse run over by the kitchen range in the kitchen and he began to stomp it as if doing a dance. He missed of course, and we haven't seen that mouse since.

CHAPTER 20

The Flood
Nell Berry 7/19/03

The flood came every spring when I was growing up in my hometown. Every year, living on the river, we would have to move out of our house and go to the courthouse till the waters receded.

Of course, this was a hardship for our families. But for the kids, it was a great adventure.

I remember the flood that year came after days of rain, coming down as if the sky had just opened up and spilled a giant bucket of water on our town.

It must have been 1934 or 1935, in that time period. For years I recalled, like a dream, hearing a large group of people singing, walking down the road outside our house. It was dark outside and it was raining. They were singing the old hymn "The Old Rugged Cross." I couldn't figure out why they would be walking down the road in the rain at night singing "The Old Rugged Cross."

Then one day I was having a discussion with my brother Wes and I asked him about it. He was a teenager at that time and he remembered the incident. He said, "That was the Salvation Army," which still didn't explain the reason for the people marching down the road singing.

I never will forget that time. The next day or so after this incident, we were forced to evacuate our home and go to the courthouse in town. There we had to sleep on the floor with several other families, on cotton mattresses, till the flood waters receded. For the parents, it was not a lot of fun. As I recall, my mother was ill at the time. So of course it was not fun at all for her. My brother Wes had to return home the next day because he needed to change his clothing. He rowed a boat into the house, right through the front door, and changed his clothes.

For the children, as I said, it was an adventure. We had a wonderful time playing in the courthouse.

Going back home after the flood waters receded was not fun, with all the mud and all our furniture and clothing having to be cleaned. It was a disaster.

We moved away from that house not long after that flood. But the next year it was the same thing for all the families that lived in that area.

Then something occurred which changed all that. They built a levee near our house where we had lived during the flood, and from that time on,there was no flood in my hometown.

BIO

I was orphaned at the age of eleven years old. If not for my brother, I don't know what would have become of me. My brother Wes was eleven years older than me. So, at the age of twenty-two he became the protector and guardian of a little sister, age eleven. He raised me and kept a roof over my head till I graduated high school. He did not have a wife to help him. He just did what he thought was right. I will be forever grateful to him.

My brother Wes is gone now. He passed away the day before Valentine's Day this year. Valentine's Day is my birthday. He was eighty-four years old. He has always been my hero, since I can remember.

I got married a week after I graduated high school. I was a mother at the age of nineteen.

Nell Berry
nmberry@mcmsys.com

Printed in the United Kingdom by
Lightning Source UK Ltd., Milton Keynes
142408UK00002B/245/A

9 781413 749717